Intro to Deer

Hunting

For Kids

Frank W Koretum

Table of Contents

Deer Hunting

You are on your first deer hunting trip with your dad, you feel both excited and nervous. You have always wanted to try deer hunting, but you have been unsure if you would be able to actually shoot a deer. However, after spending some time in the deer stand with your dad, you finally get a chance. When the deer comes into view, you take careful aim and squeeze the trigger. To your amazement, you make a perfect shot and watch as the deer falls to the ground.

ou walk up to the deer with you dad, you can hardly believe that y

it. It is a beautiful mature 11 point buck and you are so proud

self. Your dad is also excited for you and together spend the next f

ites admiring your trophy. Dad takes some pictures and then helps y

n the process of field dressing the deer. This is truly a day that you w

ys remember.

Why Deer Hunting is Good for Kids

There are many reasons why deer hunting is a good activity for kids. It teaches them responsibility, how to handle a weapon safely, and respect for nature. Additionally, it can be a bonding experience for children and parents or other family members. Hunting also provides an opportunity for kids to learn about different animal species and their habits. Overall, deer hunting is a great way for kids to learn new skills and have fun outdoors.

History of Deer Hunting

Deer hunting has been a popular sport in the United States for centuries. Early American settlers hunted deer for food and to protect their crops from damage. As the country grew, so did the popularity of deer hunting. Today, deer hunting is enjoyed by millions of people across the country every year. It is a great way to enjoy the outdoors and connect with nature. Deer hunting also plays an important role in wildlife management. By carefully regulating the harvest of deer, wildlife biologists can help ensure that populations remain healthy and sustainable.

Deer Hunting Terms

One thing that can help new hunters feel more comfortable when deer hunting is having an understanding of the words used by experienced deer hunters. The next few pages will include some of the most common terms used in deer hunting. By familiarizing yourself with these terms, you will be better prepared for your next deer hunting adventure!

Antler spread: The antler spread is the width of a buck's antlers, which can be used to determine its age and health.

Antler: The horns on a buck's head.

Bag limit: The maximum number of deer that a hunter is legally allowed to kill in one day or for the entire season.

Bed: A place where a deer rests or sleeps

Bedding area: A place where multiple deer beds are found; often used by does and their fawns

Bleating: A sound made by deer, often used to attract mates or communicate with other deer.

Blowing: When a deer makes a loud, blowing sound to warn other deer of danger

Broadside: When a deer is facing sideways in relation to the hunter, presenting a wide target.

Brow tine: The point on a buck's antlers that extends upward from the main beam.

Browsing: When a deer feeds on leaves, twigs, and buds of plants

Buck fever: Excitement or nerves felt by a hunter when they finally get a chance to shoot a deer.

Buck grunt: A call made by a buck during the rutting season to attract does.

Buck snort: A buck snort is a loud noise that male deer make during the rutting season to warn other bucks away from their territory.

Buck: A male deer.

Camouflage: Clothing worn by hunters that helps them blend in with their surroundings and avoid being seen by deer.

Can call: A device that imitates the sounds made by a doe in heat, used to attract bucks

Climbing deer stand: A type of hunting platform that is elevated and accessed by climbing stairs or a ladder.

Deer antler velvet: Deer antler velvet is the soft, furry material that covers a buck's antlers when they are in the process of growing.

Deer rubs: Scent marks that a buck will make on trees and other objects in order to mark his territory and attract does.

Deer stand: A platform that hunters use to elevate themselves above the ground, giving them a better view of the area and making it easier to shoot a deer.

Doe estrus: The period of time when a doe is receptive to mating.

Doe: A female deer.

Drive: When a group of hunters work together to push deer out of an area and towards another group of hunters who are waiting to shoot them.

Fawn: A young deer.

Feeding area: A place where multiple deer congregate to feed; often used by bucks to attract does

Field dressing: The process of removing the internal organs from a deer after it has been killed.

Fork buck: A young buck with antlers that have forked tines (points)

Funnel: An area where deer are funneled together, making them easier to spot and hunt.

Glassing: The act of scanning an area with binoculars or a spotting scope in order to find game.

Grunt tube: A device that imitates the sounds made by a buck during mating season, used to attract does

Grunting: The sound made by a buck during mating season

Gut shot: When a deer is shot in the stomach area and it is considered to be bad because the deer may suffer a long, painful death. Also, gut shots can contaminate the meat with the stomach materials from the deer.

Harvest: The taking of a deer for meat or trophy purposes.

Hunting blind: A structure that hunters can use to hide themselves from deer while they are waiting for one to come within range.

Mature: A deer that is fully grown; often used to refer to bucks with large antlers

Nubbin Buck: A young, immature male deer with very small antlers. Nubbin bucks are usually only a year or two old and have not yet reached full maturity.

Points: The projections on the antlers that are at least one inch long and one inch wide. You will often hear deer referred to by the number of points they have. Example: Jessica shot an 8 point buck.

Possession limit: The maximum number of deer that a hunter is allowed to possess at any given time

Processing: The process of butchering a deer for its meat

Quartering away: When a deer is positioned such that its quarters are facing away from the hunter, making it difficult to take a clean shot

Quartering the deer meat: Cutting the deer meat into manageable pieces for transporting or storage

Rattling: A hunting technique where the hunter clatters antlers together or uses a mechanical device to imitate the sound of fighting bucks, in order to attract does or bring bucks within range.

Rut: The mating season for deer, typically occurring in the fall.

Scent drag: A piece of cloth or other object soaked in deer urine, used to attract bucks

Scouting: The act of looking for deer in their natural habitat

Shooter: A deer that is of sufficient size and age to be harvested

Sign: Any physical evidence left by a deer, such as tracks, droppings, or rubs

Spike buck: A young buck that has not yet grown antlers with more than two points, or tines.

Spooked: When a deer is startled and runs away.

Tag: A license or permit that is required to hunt deer in most states.

Venison: The meat from a deer. Often considered a delicacy, venison is leaner and healthier than beef.

Vitals: The internal organs of a deer, located in the chest cavity; the most popular target for hunters

White flag: When a deer raises its tail as it runs, exposing the white underside, which is used as a sign of alarm or distress.

Whitetail Deer: The most common species of deer in North America.

Types of Deer

There are many different types of deer found in the United States. The most common type is the white-tailed deer, which is found in every state except Alaska. Other popular types include the mule deer, found mostly in the western states, and the black-tailed deer, found on the west coast. There are also several smaller species of deer, such as the Key deer and the Virginia deer. No matter what type of deer you are looking for, you are sure to find it in the United States.

Whitetail deer are distinguished from other types of deer by their smaller size and their white tail. The whitetail deer's coat is usually brown in color, but can vary depending on the time of year and the location.

er are distinguished from whitetail deer by their larger
ly shaped antlers. Mule deer are also known for their large ea
their name (mule = a cross between a donkey and a horse). M
rally considered to be more difficult to hunt than whitetail dee
elusive and tend to live in more remote areas. However, man
mule deer to be the most rewarding to hunt, as they provi
. If you are lucky enough to bag a mule deer, you will have
years to come!

il Deer Characteristics

er are generally herbivores, and their diet consists mos
In the winter months, when food is scarce, they will als
/hitetail deer are very adaptable creatures and can liv
nd even urban areas. They are most active at dawn ar
seen during the day.

deer mate during the fall, in what is known as the rutti

time, bucks will compete with each other for the chance to

most dominant bucks will usually mate with the most does

ant bucks may not get to mate at all. To attract does, bucks

cent-mark their territory. Once a doe has been wooed, th

then go their separate ways. After a gestation period of a

oe will give birth to one or two fawns. The fawns will stay

til they are old enough to fend for themselves, which is usu

.

Gear

In order to be successful whitetail deer hunting, you will need the proper gear. This includes a good firearm or bow, ammunition, binoculars, calls, attractants, and warm clothing. You will also need a deer stand or blind in order to get a good shot at the deer. With all of this gear, you will be able to increase your chances of bringing home a trophy whitetail deer.

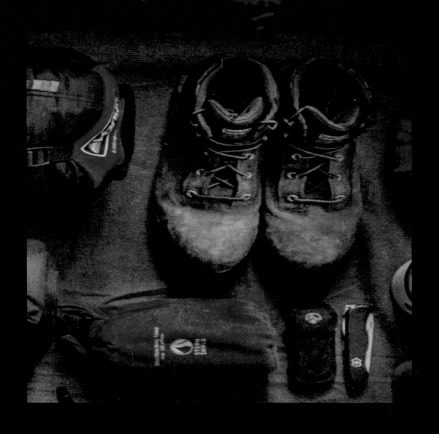

Weapon Selection

There are a variety of guns that can be used for hunting deer. Shotgu
and bows are all effective. The type of weapon that you use will depen
personal preferences and the situation that you are in. For example, i
hunting in an area with a lot of trees, you may want to use a shotgun v
designed for closer range hunting. If you are hunting in an open are
would be a better option. Bows can also be used, but require mu
practice and deer must be closer to shoot them. You must also c
regulations in your area to ensure the your weapon is legal where yo
hunt.

Rifle Selection

There are many different types of rifles that can be used for whitetail deer hunting. The most common calibers are .243, .270, and .30-06. Each caliber has its own benefits and drawbacks, so it is important to choose the one that is right for you.

The .243 is a very popular choice for deer hunting, as it is relatively light and easy to carry. It is also effective at long range, making it a good choice for open country hunting. However, the .243 is not as powerful as some of the other calibers, so it may not be the best choice if you are also planning on hunting other large game such as elk or moose.

The .270 is a good all-around caliber that is suitable for hunting both deer and elk. It is more powerful than the .243, but not as much so as the .30-06. This makes it a good choice for hunters who want a versatile rifle that can be used for multiple purposes.

The .30-06 is the most popular caliber for deer hunting, as it is very effective at long range and can take down even the largest of game animals. However, the .30-06 is also one of the heaviest calibers, so it may not be the best choice if you are planning on hiking long distances or worried about harsh recoil.

mately, the best caliber for whitetail deer hunting is the one that yo
st comfortable with. If you are new to hunting, it is a good idea to start
naller caliber such as the .243. Once you get more experience, you can r
to a larger caliber such as the .270 or .30-06. Whatever you choose, r
e that you are familiar with your rifle and confident in your ability to t
ore heading out into the field.

caliber is the diameter of the barrel on a gun. It is typically measure

meters or inches. The size of the caliber will determine the size of the b

can be fired from the gun. For example, a 9mm pistol will fire a small b

a .308 rifle will fire a much larger bullet. Different calibers are better s

ifferent purposes, so it is important to choose the right caliber for th

nd.

Shotgun Selection

There are many different types of shotguns that can be used for deer hunting including a 12 gauge and 20 gauge shotgun. A 20 gauge shotgun is a good choice for a smaller size hunters because it is lightweight and easy to handle. Additionally, a 20 gauge shotgun has less recoil than a larger 12 gauge shotgun, which makes it easier for smaller hunters to shoot and less scary for a new hunter to use. Always make sure to check local hunting regulations to ensure you are using the size of gun that is legal for deer hunting in your area.

gauge of a shotgun refers to the diameter of the barrel. The most comm
ges are 12, 16, 20, and 28. The higher the number, the smaller the diame
he barrel. A 12 gauge shotgun has a larger barrel than a 20 gauge shotg
s means that a 12 gauge shotgun typically has more power than a 20 ga
tgun. However, the power a 12 gauge shotgun has more recoil than a
ge shotgun making it less friendly for inexperienced hunters.

Adding a scope to your shotgun or rifle can help magnify the deer, which make it easier to shoot them. The most popular scope is the 3 x 9, which m that it makes the deer appear 3 times closer when set at the 3 setting a times closer when set on the 9 setting. This is a good all-purpose scope tha be used for hunting in various conditions. If you plan on doing a lot of hunting, investing in a good quality scope is worth the money.

Bow Selection

A compound bow is a type of bow that uses pulleys and cables to store energy, which allows it to be much more powerful than a traditional bow. This makes it ideal for deer hunting, as it increases the chances of taking down a deer with one shot. However, there are some drawbacks to using a compound bow for deer hunting.

First, they can be more expensive than traditional bows. Second, they can be difficult to use if you are not experienced with them. If you are looking for a challenge and are willing to invest the time and money into learning how to use a compound bow, then it can be an incredibly rewarding experience.

Most bowhunters use broadhead arrows for deer hunting. Broadhead arrows have a wider head than traditional arrows, and they are designed to cause more damage when they hit an animal. Most hunters use arrows with carbon or aluminum shafts. Carbon shafts are lighter and faster than aluminum shafts, but they are also more expensive. Aluminum shafts are not as fast as carbon shafts, but they are less likely to break on impact.

There are many different types of broadhead arrows, so it is important to choose one that is best suited for your hunting style. If you are new to bowhunting, it is d idea to talk to an experienced hunter or visit a local archery shop

advice on what type of arrow to use. No matter what type of arro

e, remember that practice makes perfect! The more you shoot, the

chances of success when deer season rolls around.

Licensing

A hunting license is required in most states in order to hunt deer. A hunting license ensures that hunters are knowledgeable about hunting regulations and safety. Additionally, a hunting license helps to fund conservation efforts and wildlife management programs.

gulations

e are many regulations on deer hunting including the seasons that you
deer and the limit of deer you can shoot in one day. The season for
ing typically runs from the fall through middle of the winter. Be su
the exact season dates for where you are hunting.

Bag Limits

In most states, the typical bag limit for whitetail deer is one or two per hunter. This means that each hunter is legally allowed to kill one or two whitetail deer in one day or over the course of the entire hunting season. Some states have different bag limits depending on the area you are hunting in or the time of year, so it is always best to check with your local wildlife department before heading out.

Regardless of the bag limit, all hunters should be mindful of their impact on the local deer population and only take what they will use. Deer populations can fluctuate greatly from year to year, so it is important to only harvest what you need in order to ensure a healthy population for years to come.

Hunters Education and Safety

Many states require hunters to go through a hunters education course in
to hunt. These courses teach hunters about hunting regulations and s
Additionally, many of these courses can now be done online. After a certai
the course might not be required. However, even if the course is not req
these courses are still beneficial for hunters to learn about hunting safet
regulations.

When deer hunting, there are multiple forms of hunter safety to be aware of. Always keep your gun on safe or arrows in your quiver until you are ready to shoot. Always keep your weapon pointed in a safe direction and ensure that you identify what you are shooting at before you shoot. Also identify what is behind where you are shooting to ensure that you do not hit another person or buildings. Following these safety guidelines will help ensure that everyone has an enjoyable and safe deer hunting experience.

What to Wear

If you are planning on hunting whitetail deer, there are a few things you will need to take into consideration when it comes to your clothing. For starters, you will want to make sure that you wear clothing that will help you stay warm and comfortable. You might also want to consider investing in some camouflage clothing, as this can be helpful in hiding from the deer. In addition to camouflage clothing, many states require hunters to wear a blaze orange vest and hat during firearm seasons. This is because blaze orange is a highly visible color that helps other hunters spot you from a distance, preventing accidental shootings. However, during bow hunting seasons, blaze orange is usually not required.

Preparing for Emergencies

When deer hunting, it is important to be prepared in case of an emergency. Hunters should bring a compass, cell phone, map, hunting knife and fire starter with them. These items will help hunters if they get lost or stranded. Additionally, hunters should tell someone where they are going and when they plan to return. This way if you get lost or injured someone knows where to come and find you.

od to Bring

en deer hunting, it is a good idea to pack food that will not spoil and that you energy. Some good options include beef jerky, granola bars, sandwic water. It is also a good idea to pack more food than you think you will n se you get lost or stranded.

Where to Hunt

There are a few different ways that you can find good places to hunt deer. The first way is to ask around. Talk to other hunters and see if they have any suggestions for good hunting spots. Another way to find good hunting spots is to do some research online. There are many websites and forums that are dedicated to hunting, and you can find a wealth of information on where to find the best hunting spots. You can always ask the local game warden for advice. They will be able to tell you where the best hunting spots are and what time of year is best for hunting in those areas.

One of the best ways to find deer to hunt is to spend time in a vehicle driving around looking for them. These animals are often found in remote areas, and they can be difficult to find. The best way to scout for these animals is to drive around country roads and look for signs of deer and good habitat for them to roam. If you see one in a field that can be a great place to speak to the owner and see if you can hunt there.

Whitetail deer tracks are relatively easy to identify, as they are oval-shaped with three distinct toes. The middle toe is usually the longest and most pronounced. Whitetail deer tracks typically measure between 2-3 inches long and 1-2 inches wide. If you see a set of tracks that meet these criteria, there is a good chance that they were made by a whitetail deer.

It is also important to note how old the deer tracks are. One way to tell how old deer tracks are is by looking at the edges of the tracks. Tracks with deep sharp edges are likely to be newer tracks maybe made in the last 24 hours. However, tracks with soft and round edges are probably at least a few days old.

You can also determine how large or small the deer was that left the tracks. Large and deep hoof prints could be a mature buck where smaller shallow tracks could be does or young deer. By carefully examining deer tracks, you can get a good idea of what kind of deer you are dealing with and how long ago it was in the area.

Deer antler rubs are made when a deer rubs its antlers on a tree. This is done for a few reasons: to mark their territory, to shed the velvet from their antlers, and to attract does. All of these are good signs to know that a mature buck is in the area. You can tell how old a deer rub is by looking at the marks on the tree. If the rubs still have some green on them, then they are likely within the last day. However, if the marks are all dark brown, it means the rub was done a few days ago.

When to Hunt

The best time of day to hunt whitetail deer is at sunrise and sunset. This is when the deer are most active and thus more likely to be seen by hunters. Most states have laws that prohibit hunting during the hours of darkness, so it is important to make sure you are familiar with the regulations in your state before heading out. In general, the legal hunting time is 1/2 hour before sunrise to 1/2 hour after sunset.

Ways to Hunt

There are many different techniques that can be used to hunt whitetail deer, but some of the most popular include the spot and stalk, waiting in a deer stand, and going on deer drives. The spot and stalk involves finding a deer and then stalking it until you are within range to shoot it. This can be difficult, as deer are very good at spotting predators and will often run away before you have a chance to get close.

Waiting in a deer stand is another popular technique, where hunters will set up a platform in an area where they know deer will be passing through and wait for one to come within range. Deer drives are when a group of hunters work together to push deer out of an area and towards another group of hunters who are waiting to shoot them. This can be an effective way to bag a deer, but it requires good coordination and communication between all of the hunters involved. Let's discuss each of these techniques a little more.

and Stalk

d stalk is a hunting technique that is used to hunt whitetail de
looks for deer from a distance and then stalks closer to the anim
e within range to shoot. This technique requires a lot of patien
as the deer will easily spook if they see or hear the hunter comi
cessful spot and stalking include choosing the right time of day (c
using binoculars or a spotting scope to find deer from a distan
g camouflage clothing to help you blend in with your surrounding
ster the art of spot and stalk, you will be sure to have succes
g whitetail deer.

Deer Stand Hunting

One of the most popular techniques for hunting whitetail deer is to wait in a deer stand. A deer stand is a platform that hunters use to elevate themselves above the ground, giving them a better view of the area and making it easier to shoot a deer. Many deer stands are located near food or water sources, as deer often come to these areas to eat and drink.

When waiting in a deer stand, it is important to be patient and remain still. If a deer does not come within range after a few hours, do not be discouraged – sometimes it can take all day for one to finally appear. Remember to dress warmly, as you will likely be sitting in the same spot for an extended period of time. And always be sure to have your gun ready and safety on, as you never know when a deer will finally show up! With a little patience and luck, you will be able to bag the prize whitetail deer that you have been dreaming of.

When hunting from a deer stand, safety is of the utmost importance. You should always unload your gun when climbing on and off your stand, and use a shoulder sling or rope to bring the gun up to the stand. You should also wear a harness while in the stand to ensure you do not fall out. By taking these precautions, you can help avoid accidents and injuries while enjoying your time deer hunting.

Deer Sense of Smell

Deer are extremely sensitive to smell and even the slightest human
cause them to flee an area. For this reason, it is important to ta
precaution to eliminate human smells when deer hunting. This includ
your hunting clothes to hang outside for about a week prior to deer h
ensure all human smell is gone. Then, on the day of your hunt, you can
eliminator spray to help get rid of any last smells that remain. If you fa
of this and the deer get wind of you, they will quickly flee the area,
harder for you to find them. However, if you are able to successfully r
human scent, you will have a much better chance of bagging that trop

Deer scents can be used to attract bucks during the rutting season. One way to do this is to buy a deer scent that smells like doe urine and put it on deer rubs. This will make the bucks think a female has stopped by, letting them know she is interested in mating with him. Another way to use deer scents is to put some on your clothes or gear. This will help you blend in with your surroundings and make you less likely to be detected by the deer. Finally, you can put some on fabric wicks that usually come with the purchase of deer scents and then hang this on a tree branch so that the smell can travel a long distance

Deer Drives

A deer drive is when a group of hunters work together to push deer out of an area and towards another group of hunters who are waiting to shoot them. Deer drives can be very successful in getting deer to move into an area where they can be more easily hunted, but they must be done carefully and with safety in mind. All hunters involved in a deer drive must be aware of the location of all other hunters at all times, as there is a danger of being shot if you are not careful.

Deer Calls & Antler Rattles

can be a helpful tool when deer hunting, as they can attr
on. There are many different types of deer calls, including
bleat calls, and even rattling deer antlers together to re
o bucks fighting. Using a deer calls or antler rattles can hel
ange, giving you a better chance of making a successful s
using deer calls, it is best to practice in your backyard or s
on before heading out into the woods. This way yo
e with the call and increase your chances of success
s around.

t place to aim when shooting a deer is in the heart or lungs. These are all

ans that, if hit, will quickly kill the deer. This is important for two reasons:

u want to ensure a quick and humane kill; and second, you don't want

r to run off and die somewhere where it could be difficult to find it and

ve to deal with tracking it for hours.

When you shoot a deer, it is important to give it time to die and bleed out. This usually takes about 30 minutes. If you try to find the deer too soon, it may still be alive and you could scare it further away, which will only make it harder to find. Additionally, deer often travel in groups, so if you shoot one deer, there is a good chance that another deer is not far behind. Giving the deer time to bleed out will ensure that you have waited for any other deer in the area to come into your line of sight.

When tracking a wounded deer, the first thing you need to do is find the spot where you shot it. Look for signs of blood on leaves, branches, and dirt. If the blood is bright red, it means the deer is not far ahead of you. If it is dark red or brown, it means the deer has been bedded down for a while and you may have to do some more serious tracking. But if you follow the blood, eventually you will find your deer. It is also a good idea to leave some type of marker on the last spot you found blood in case you lose the trail you can go back to that spot and start looking again.

...g Your Game

...hoot a deer, it is very important to field dress it as soon a...
...es removing the internal organs from the deer so that t...
...compose and contaminate the meat. Depending on whe...
...ou may be able to take the deer to a butcher or processi...
...one for you. However, if you are in a remote area, you v...
...elf. There are many instructional videos and articles avail...
...ow you how to properly field dress a deer. Once the d...
...is important to get it into a cool storage facility as soon as...
...eat does not spoil.

After you skin a deer, you can donate the hide to programs like Hides for H

These programs sell the hides to fur buyers and the proceeds are used f

conservation efforts. Many local gas stations are drop off sites for these t

programs and often give you some type of gift for donating hides, such a

of gloves or hunting knives. This is a great way to help support deer conse

efforts and ensure that these magnificent animals will be around for

generations to enjoy.

oking Deer

e are many different ways to cook venison, and the best way to co
nds on your personal preferences. Some people like to simply grill
venison, while others prefer to have it made into brats, hot dogs, or po
. If you are worried about the gamey taste of venison, you can always
a butcher to have it made into these products. Many people who
on tastes gamey still find that they enjoy it when it is processed this v

...vation

...ng is an important part of wildlife conservation in North America. By ...anaging the deer population, we can ensure that future generations ... to enjoy these magnificent animals. One way that hunters can help ...vation is by picking up any garbage that they see in the woods. This ...ings like empty ammunition shells and empty deer attractant ... Hunters should also only shoot the number of deer that they will ..., as this helps to prevent waste. Finally, hunters can help to improve ...t by planting food plots and other vegetation that will provide shelter ...r deer. By taking these steps, we can ensure that deer populations ...lthy for years to come.

ap

hunting is a great sport for kids because it teaches responsibility, respect for nature. Additionally, it can be a bonding experience be en and their parents or other family members. The excitement of sh first deer is unparalleled; it's an exhilarating feeling that will stay with er. Deer hunting is a great way to have fun outdoors while learnin and connecting with the environment. Overall, deer hunting is an exc y for kids of all ages.

Made in United States
Orlando, FL
23 December 2022

27547857R00031